TRIO A DOG'S TAIL

A True Story About A Homeless Three-Legged Dog

Written by

Chris Mohler and Ross Singer

Illustrated by

Cherri L. Neal

Chris and Ross would like to acknowledge the following people:

Jenny Augustin for her emotional support, and without whose help this book would not have been created.

Joanna King editing support.

Andy Williams for his technical support.

Once upon a time on the outskirts of a city not far away, lived a little Chihuahua dog. No one, not even he, was sure where his home was. Every night he slept wherever he could find shelter.

TRIO, A DOG'S TAIL

One day two young boys found him sleeping under their trailer. They thought it would be fun to put him on the roof of the trailer. The little dog got scared and jumped off the roof. The boys ran away when they saw the little dog was hurt. His poor, little leg had broken when he jumped.

For many years, he had to fend for himself even though his leg hurt all the time because it hadn't healed right. But the little Chihuahua was blessed; even with a broken leg he could run very fast.

Years later, he was running through a field when a friendly Animal Control Officer spotted him.

TRIO, A DOG'S TAIL

She had very yummy treats and the little dog was SO hungry, he ran right up to her. She hugged him hard, and she promised the little dog that she would take him to a special place where they would make sure he would be safe and find a forever home.

She took him to a big Animal Shelter with loving people who are very good at helping dogs and cats find homes where they would always be loved. The doctors there were very smart.

They knew for him to live a long and healthy life, his bad leg would have to be removed. Instead of four legs he would now have only three.

TRIO, A DOG'S TAIL

4-12-17 Cherri

The doctors there named him TRIO, which is a word you can use when you're talking about three things or three people. Trio had three legs, so it seemed like a good name for him.

Trio found a loving family who took him home. His new family had other Chihuahuas and a boy and girl to play with. They ran, jumped, and played fetch all day.

TRIO, A DOG'S TAIL

One day a movie director called Trio's family. He was looking for dogs with three legs to be in a movie. The director met Trio and fell in love with him. He made him the star of the movie.

Trio worked very hard and was proud of his role in the movie. You see, Trio figured out that he could do anything with his 3 legs that a dog with 4 legs could do. Trio learned that it doesn't matter if you look different from others. You can still accomplish anything you set your heart on doing.

Trio the Chihuahua became famous and children everywhere fell in love with the little dog with 3 legs. Trio showed everyone all over the world that with love and determination you can live happily ever after just like him!

Color this picture of Trio

THE END

But not for Trio....

Be on the lookout for the next adventures of Trio.

78255842R00018

Made in the USA
Lexington, KY
06 January 2018